MW01000106

Sewing
Season's Greetings™

Designs by Carol Zentgraf

HOUSE of
WHITE
BIRCHES

PUBLISHERS
SINCE 1947

Sewing Season's Greetings

I love Christmas—everything about it, from decorating to gift giving to entertaining friends and family. If you do too, then *Sewing Season's Greetings* is for you. Inside, you'll find more than 30 projects designed to suit a variety of tastes and every sewing skill level.

If the first thing on your holiday agenda is decorating your home, you'll be sure to love the yummy array of felt "sweet treats" ornaments for trimming the tree, the Whimsical Tree Skirt & Stocking, and the Holly Candle Mat with its dimensional leaves. The yo-yo wreath and throw are easy to make using your favorite cotton prints or stitch the snowflake fleece throw and pillow to add a cozy touch to your decor. If you're looking for elegant accents, the Elegant Stripes Mantel Cloth & Pillow, as well as the Richly Jeweled Runner are beautiful when made with gorgeous fabrics and trims.

Planning a party or want to set a festive table for holiday meals? Look no further than the Fun & Festive Table Ensemble, complete with a table runner, place mats, napkin rings and even a tea cozy. The polka-dot place mats with their coordinating stocking silverware holders add a touch of fun to your table. The Dress Up Your Table tablecloth can be made to fit any size table. The Santa coasters, appliquéd tea towels and casserole caddies are practical as well as festive.

When it comes to gift giving, nothing is more special than a gift you made yourself. The sweatshirt jacket and soft wallet with a detachable strap are perfect for giving, but you may want to make one of each for yourself as well. The embossed velvet bag is ideal for using as a gift bag or for holding a bottle of wine to take to a party as a hostess gift. Of course you don't want to forget your favorite pup either—we've even included a Santa coat with coordinating booties and a leash.

I hope you will have as much fun making these projects as I did designing them. Happy holidays and happy sewing!

Carol

Table of Contents

Holly Candle Mat,
page 12

Richly Jeweled
*Runner, **page 25***

Polka Dots & Stripes
*Table Set, **page 38***

*Ribbon & Ornament Tea Towels, **page 45***

House of White Birches, Berne, Indiana 46711   DRGnetwork.com

Sweet Treats Ornaments

No baking is required for this assortment of sweet treats to trim a tree or use as party favors.

Finished Sizes
Smallest: 3 x 3 inches
Largest: 3 x 5 inches

Materials for All Ornaments
- 7 inches ⅛-inch-wide ribbon for each hanger
- 6mm and 4mm heat-set crystals in assorted colors
- Heat-set crystal wand applicator
- Polyester fiberfill
- Permanent fabric adhesive
- Basic sewing supplies and equipment

Additional Materials for Each Ornament
Note: See templates on pages 7 and 8 for scrap sizes.

Gingerbread Man
- Scrap light brown wool felt
- Baby rickrack:
    ¼ yard white
    1 inch red

Hard Candy
- Scrap white wool felt
- 9 inches puprle regular rickrack
- Ribbon:
    3½ inches ⅜-inch-wide
    24 inches ⅛-inch-wide

Candy Cane
- Scrap white wool felt
- Rickrack:
    5 inches red regular
    9 inches red baby
- 8 inches ⅜-inch-wide ribbon

Lollipop
- Scraps red and white wool felt
- ¼ yard red baby rickrack
- ⅜-inch flat white button
- ½ yard ⅜-inch-wide ribbon

Mitten No. 1
- Scraps purple, light green and light pink wool felt
- 8 inches ⅜-inch-wide ribbon

Mitten No. 2
- Scraps bright pink, light pink and dark green wool felt
- Brass ⅜-inch heat-set star

Cupcake
- Scraps light green and pink wool felt
- 5 inches ⅛-inch-wide ribbon

Gingerbread Man, Hard Candy, Candy Cane & Lollipop Ornaments
Cutting

From light brown wool felt:
- Use template to cut one front and one back for gingerbread man ornament.

From white wool felt:
- Use templates to cut one front and one back each for hard candy, candy cane and lollipop ornaments.
- Cut a 1 x 4-inch strip for lollipop stick.

From red wool felt:
- Use template to cut lollipop sections.

Assembly

1. Glue ends of each 7-inch ribbon hanger together to form a loop. Set aside.

2. Place lollipop sections evenly spaced around lollipop front and stitch in place.

3. Using photos as a guide, embellish ornament fronts by cutting rickrack and/or ribbon to fit, then edgestitching in place.

4. Fold strip of felt for lollipop stick in half lengthwise and stitch. Insert end of stick between lollipop front and back. Adhere with a dab of glue.

5. Insert glued ends of ribbon loop between front and back at top of each ornament. Adhere with a dab of glue.

6. Insert a small amount of fiberfill between front and back of each ornament, then stitch front and back together ⅛ inch from edges. **Note:** *It may be easier to sew edges together partially around ornament, then stuff before completely closing edges.*

7. Finish embellishing with ribbon bows and heat-set crystals as shown in photos.

Mitten No. 1, Mitten No. 2 & Cupcake Ornaments

Cutting

From purple wool felt:
• Use mitten template to cut one front and one back for mitten No. 1 ornament.

From bright pink wool felt:
• Use mitten template to cut one front and one back for mitten No. 2 ornament.

From light pink wool felt:
• Use mitten cuff template to cut one front and one back for mitten No. 2.

Tips & Techniques

These ornaments are a perfect way to use up some of those treasures in your scrap bag. Every sewer has one—filled with bits and pieces of ribbon, trim, buttons, lace and other embellishments we bought for former projects and just couldn't throw away! So dig into your leftover treasures before you head to the fabric store.

• Use cupcake top template to cut one front and one back for cupcake.
• Use heart template to cut one appliqué for mitten No. 1.

From light green wool felt:
• Use mitten cuff template to cut one front and one back for mitten No. 1.
• Use cupcake bottom template to cut one front and one back for cupcake.

From dark green wool felt:
• Use tree template to cut one appliqué for mitten No. 2.

Assembly

1. Glue ends of each 7-inch ribbon hanger together to form a loop. Set aside.

2. For each mitten, sew front cuff to front mitten. Repeat with back cuff and back mitten, making sure back mittens mirror front mittens. Sew heart appliqué to front of mitten No. 1; sew tree appliqué to front of mitten No. 2.

3. Using photo as a guide, cut and stitch ribbons to front of cupcake bottom. Sew front of cupcake top to cupcake bottom. Sew cupcake back top and bottom together, making sure they mirror cupcake front.

4. Insert glued ends of ribbon loops inside top edges of mittens and tip of cupcake between fronts and back. Adhere with a dab of glue.

5. Sew cupcake bottom together ⅛ inch from edges. Lightly stuff cupcake and complete sewing around cupcake top.

6. Finish embellishing with ribbon bow on mitten No. 1, and heat-set crystals and star as shown in photo. ❖

Sources: *Wool Felt squares from National Nonwovens; ribbon from May Arts; Kandi Kane applicator wand and heat-set crystals from Kandi Corp.; polyester fiberfill from Fairfield Processing; Fabri-Tac permanent fabric adhesive from Beacon Adhesives.*

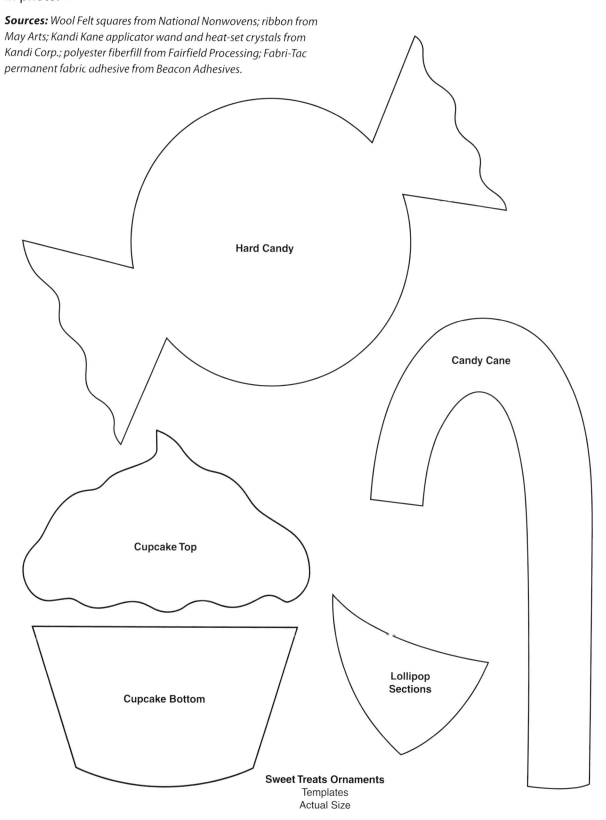

Hard Candy

Candy Cane

Cupcake Top

Cupcake Bottom

Lollipop Sections

Sweet Treats Ornaments
Templates
Actual Size

House of White Birches, Berne, Indiana 46711   DRGnetwork.com

Gingerbread Man

Heart

Tree

Mitten Cuff

Lollipop Top

Mitten

Sweet Treats Ornaments
Templates
Actual Size

Fleece Snowflake Set

These snowflakes won't chill your toes! They will keep you warm and cozy when you appliqué them on a snuggly fleece throw and matching pillow.

Finished Sizes
Throw: 50 x 60 inches
Pillow: 18 x 18 inches

Materials
• 60-inch-wide fleece fabric:
   2 yards red
   1 yard white
• 18 x 18-inch pillow form
• 2½ yards 1½-inch-wide white ball fringe with header tape
• Self-adhesive double-sided basting tape
• 12-weight white cotton thread
• Optional: permanent fabric adhesive
• 15 x 30-inch piece freezer paper
• Basic sewing supplies and equipment

Freezer-Paper Snowflake Pattern
• Cut two 15 x 15-inch pieces of freezer paper. Fold each square in half, then in half again.

• Trace or photocopy the large/small snowflake template on page 10. Align the corner of template with one folded freezer-paper corner and cut out the large snowflake pattern. Unfold snowflake pattern.

• Repeat with remaining freezer-paper to cut out small snowflake pattern.

• When ready to use, place the snowflake pattern wax side down on the fleece. Using a press cloth and a dry iron set on medium-low heat, press to adhere the pattern to the fleece. **Note:** *Do not touch the iron directly on the fleece.*

• Cut fleece along pattern lines using a rotary point cutter and mat, or sharp-pointed scissors. Remove the snowflake pattern and repeat process to make additional snowflakes.

Cutting
From red fleece:
• Cut one 50 x 60-inch panel for throw.
• Cut two 18½ x 18½-inch squares for pillow front and back.

From white fleece:
Note: Follow instructions at left to make snowflake patterns from freezer paper.

• Use large pattern to cut three large snowflakes for the throw and one large snowflake for the pillow.
• Use small pattern to cut five small snowflakes for the throw.

Assembly
Use a ¼-inch seam allowance unless otherwise noted.

1. Place the fleece throw on a large flat surface. Arrange three large and five small snowflakes on the throw as desired. Carefully lift up each arm of each snowflake and apply a strip of basting tape along the center of the arm on the wrong side. Remove the paper backing and adhere the arm to the throw.

Tips & Techniques
Fleece is an easy fabric to work with.

• Cut edges do not fray. You can finish cut edges with decorative machine or hand stitches—as in this project—or by using specialty scissors that create scalloped or other decorative edges.

• Always use a press cloth and medium-low heat on fleece. High, direct heat will leave imprints and sometimes melt fleece.

2. Center the remaining large snowflake on one pillow panel and adhere with basting tape in the same manner.

3. Use 12-weight cotton thread and a blanket stitch to stitch around the edges of each snowflake and the edges of the throw (Figure 1).

4. With the ball fringe toward the center, pin and baste the inside edge of the header tape ¼ inch from the fleece edge of the appliquéd pillow front. Sew the pillow front and back with right sides together, leaving a 9-inch opening in the center of one edge. Turn right side out and insert the pillow form. Slipstitch the opening closed.

5. Cut the balls from the leftover ball fringe. Randomly stitch or glue to the throw. ❖

Sources: *Soft Touch pillow insert from Fairfield Processing; 12-weight cotton thread from Sulky of America; Fabri-Tac permanent fabric adhesive from Beacon Adhesives.*

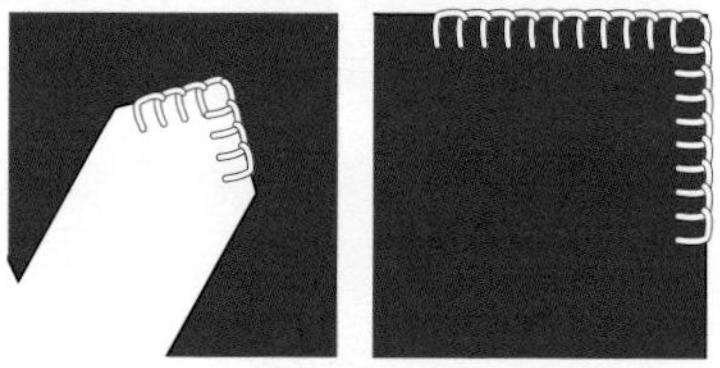

Figure 1

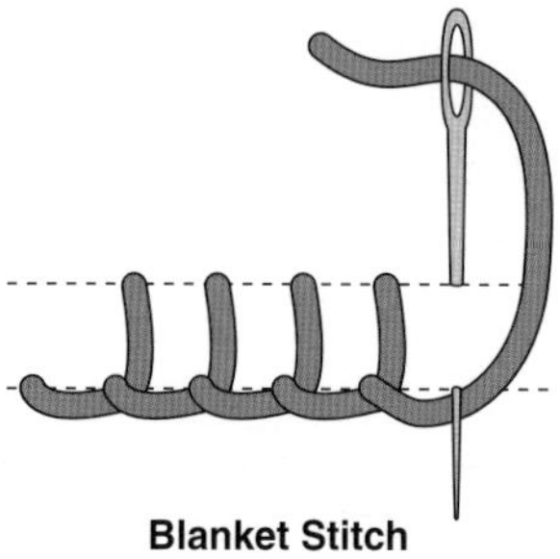

Blanket Stitch

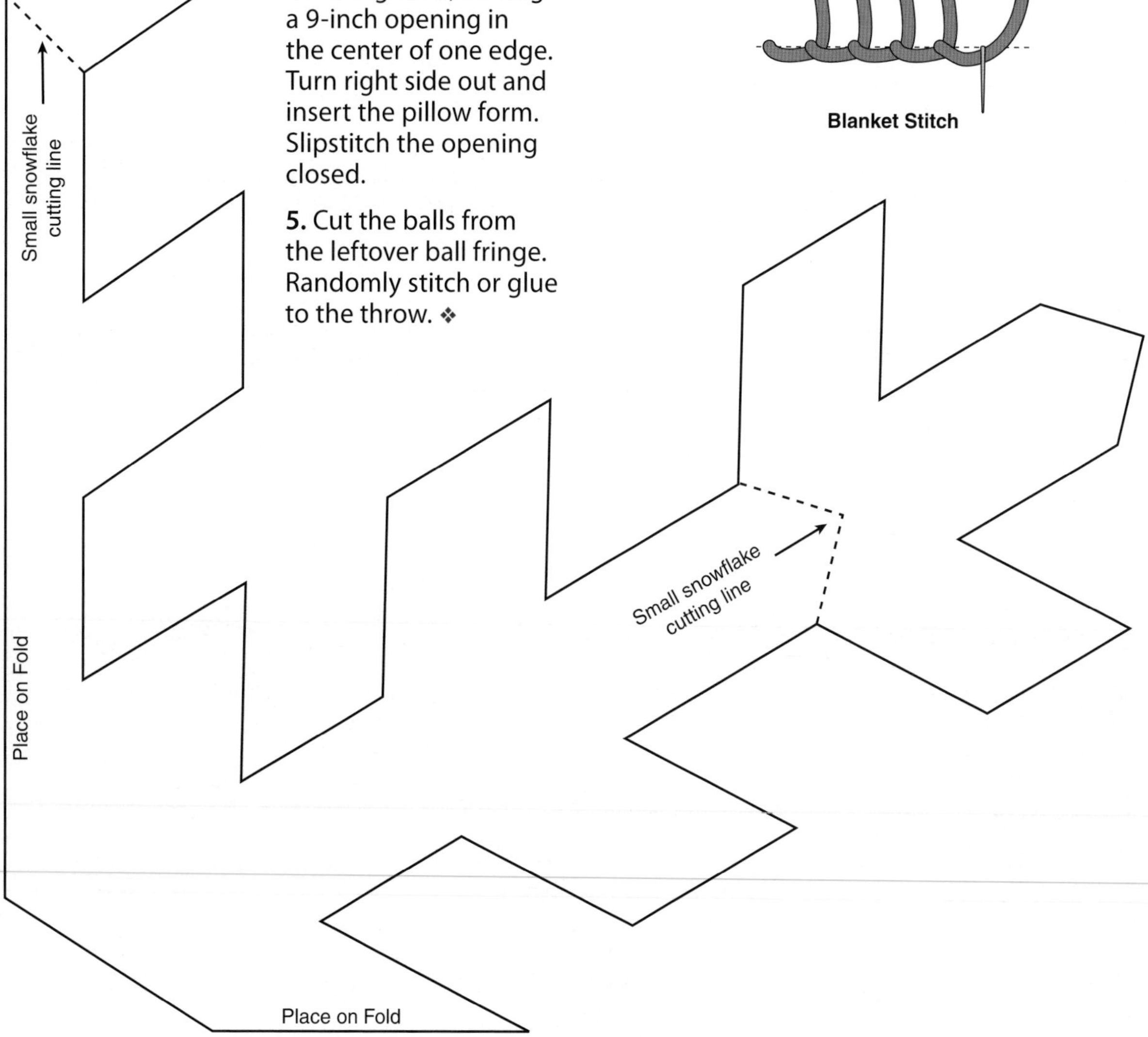

Small snowflake cutting line

Place on Fold

Small snowflake cutting line

Place on Fold

Fleece Snowflake Set
Template
Actual Size

Holly Candle Mat

A 3-inch-diameter pillar candle or candle jar sits perfectly in the center of this mat surrounded by soft-sculpture holly leaves.

Finished Size
7½ inches in diameter

Materials
- 44/45-inch-wide cotton fabric:
    - ¼ yard medium- to heavyweight red
    - ¼ yard green print
    - ⅛ yard red print
- Small amount polyester fiberfill
- Yo-yo maker to make extra-small (¾-inch) yo-yos
- Optional: permanent fabric adhesive
- Basic sewing supplies and equipment

Cutting
From medium- to heavyweight red:
- Cut two 6¼-inch-diameter circles for mat.

From green print:
- Cut two 9 x 22-inch rectangles for holly leaves.

From red print:
- Using extra-small yo-yo maker, cut 9 circles for holly berries.

Assembly
Sew right sides together using a ¼-inch seam allowance unless otherwise noted.

1. Sew mat circles together, leaving an opening for turning. Turn right side out; press. Slipstitch opening closed.

2. Layer holly leaves rectangles right sides together; pin. Trace holly leaf template 11 times onto layered fabric, spacing at least ½ inch apart. Sew on traced lines.

3. Cut out each leaf ⅛ inch beyond stitching lines and cut a ¾-inch slit through one layer of fabric. Turn right side out through opening; press.

4. Lightly stuff each leaf with fiberfill. Slipstitch or glue opening closed. On opposite side of each leaf, stitch a vein down the middle as shown on template.

5. Follow yo-yo maker instructions to make nine yo-yos from red-print circles.

6. Referring to photo, arrange holly leaves around mat, overlapping slightly, and pin. Hand-tack each leaf to mat with matching thread. Arrange yo-yo berries as desired and tack with matching thread. ❖

Source: *Extra-small yo-yo maker #8702 from Clover Needlecraft Inc.*

Tips & Techniques
Adjust the size of the mat circle and the number of leaves to make mat fit a larger or smaller candle or jar.

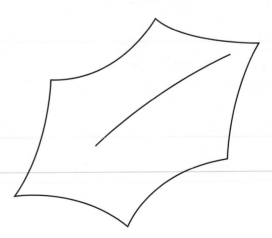

Holly Candle Mat
Holly Leaf Template
Actual Size

Yo-Yo Christmas Throw

Add a joyful spot to your holiday home with this easy throw made with giant-size yo-yos.

Finished Size
40 x 50 inches

Materials
- 44-inch-wide cotton fabric:
    3 yards total assorted green prints, each at least ⅓ yard in length
    4 yards total assorted red prints each at least ⅓ yard in length
- Basic sewing supplies and equipment

Cutting
From green prints:
- Cut 32 (11-inch-diamter) circles.

From red prints:
- Cut 48 (11-inch-diameter) circles.

Assembly
1. Press under the edge of each circle ½ inch to wrong side.

2. Thread a hand-sewing needle with a double length of matching all-purpose thread. Make a gathering stitch around the edge of each circle through the ½-inch hem, close to the fold.

3. Pull thread to gather edge to a ½-inch-diameter opening. Knot thread ends to secure.

4. Position opening in center top of each yo-yo and finger-press edges.

5. On large flat surface, arrange green yo-yos to form a border 10 yo-yos long and eight wide. Fill center with six rows of eight red print yo-yos. Hand-stitch yo-yos together with matching thread. ❖

Source: *Fabrics from Robert Kauffman Fabrics.*

House of White Birches, Berne, Indiana 46711   DRGnetwork.com

Yo-Yo Wreath

Decorate your door with this fun and festive yo-yo wreath.

Finished Size
Approximately 12 inches in diameter

Materials
- 44-inch-wide cotton fabric:
    - 1½ yards total assorted green and red prints for yo-yos
    - ½ yard green print to wrap wreath
- 12-inch-diameter plastic foam wreath form
- Yo-yo maker to make large (2½-inch) yo-yos
- Permanent fabric adhesive
- Basic sewing supplies and equipment

Cutting
From assorted green and red prints for yo-yos:
- Cut 58 (6-inch-diamter) circles.

From green print to wrap wreath:
- Cut seven 2-inch-wide strips across the width of the fabric.

Assembly
1. Glue one end of one 2-inch strip to the back of the plastic foam wreath. Wrap strip around wreath and glue opposite end to the back. Repeat with remaining strips to cover surface of wreath.

2. Follow yo-yo maker's instructions to make 58 yo-yos from 6-inch-diameter circles.

3. Arrange 24 yo-yos in a single layer on outside edge of wreath, overlapping edges. Carefully lift each yo-yo and glue in place.

4. Repeat step 3 to glue 14 yo-yos around inside edge of wreath and 20 yo-yos over the front of the wreath. Let glue dry. ❖

Sources: *Fabrics from RJR Fabrics; yo-yo maker from Clover Needlecraft Inc.; Fabri-Tac permanent fabric adhesive from Beacon Adhesives.*

Whimsical Tree Skirt & Stocking

Add a touch of whimsy to your holiday decor with the bright colors of fun-loving print and stripe fabrics combined with coordinating trim and tassels.

Finished Sizes
Stocking: 11 x 18 inches
Tree Skirt: 65 inches in diameter

Materials
- 44-inch-wide cotton fabric:
    4⅛ yards Christmas print
    3 yards white tonal
    1½ yards stripe
- 30 inches 22-inch-wide fusible interfacing
- 4 yards red pin-dot double-fold bias trim
- 2½ yards ⅛-inch-wide ribbon for skirt
- 8 (4½-inch) red tassels for skirt
- 1¼ yards ½-inch-wide red gimp trim for stocking
- 1 yard Christmas beaded trim with header for stocking
- 9 x 12-inch sheet paper-backed fusible web
- Permanent fabric adhesive
- Basic sewing supplies and equipment

Tree Skirt
Cutting
Refer to tree skirt panel and tree skirt point templates on page 21 to draw the patterns on pattern tracing paper or cloth. Cut out patterns.

From Christmas print:
- Cut eight tree skirt panels.

From white tonal:
- Cut two 68-inch-long panels the width of fabric for backing.

From stripe:
- Cut eight tree skirt points.

From ⅛-inch-wide ribbon:
- Cut eight 11-inch lengths.

Assembly
Sew seams with right sides together using a ¼-inch seam allowance unless otherwise noted.

1. Matching centers, sew a point to the end of each panel (Figure 1).

Figure 1   Figure 2

2. Sew side edges of panels together, using a ½-inch seam allowance, leaving one seam open (Figure 2). Press seams open.

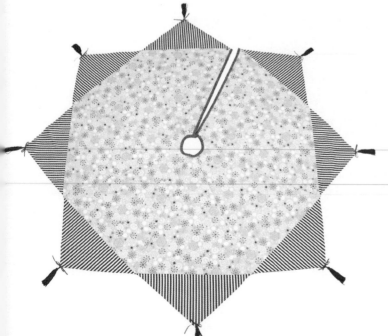

3. Sew the long edges of the backing panels together and press the seam open. Pin assembled top to backing with right sides together and the backing seam centered. Trim backing to match top (Figure 3). Sew lower edges together, leaving center back edges and curved center hole unstitched. Turn right side out and press.

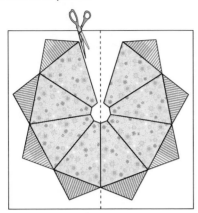

Figure 3

4. Cut the center opening larger, if desired, to fit tree stand. Baste the skirt and lining edges together along the open seams and center.

5. Cut two strips of bias trim the length of the unstitched panels plus 1 inch. Open bias trim flat at short ends, fold ½ inch of short ends to wrong side and press. Refold trim and press (Figure 4). Center bias trim over basted edges and edgestitch (Figure 5).

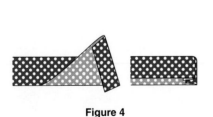

Figure 4

Figure 5

6. Cut a strip of bias trim 16 to 20 inches longer than the center opening. Prepare the bias trim as in step 5 (Figure 4). Center the bias trim over the center opening and edgestitch in place. Continue edgestitching to sew the open edges of the extending trim ends together.

7. Center a tassel loop on each 11-inch length of ribbon and tie ribbon into a bow. Stitch or glue to the ends of tree skirt points.

Stocking

Cutting

Refer to stocking, toe and cuff templates on facing page to draw the patterns on pattern tracing paper or cloth. Cut out patterns.

From Christmas print:
• Cut four stockings, reversing two.

From stripe:
• Cut four cuffs, reversing two.
• Trace two toes (reversing one) onto paper backing of fusible web. Cut out just outside traced lines and fuse onto wrong side of fabric. Cut out on traced lines. Set aside.

From fusible interfacing:
• Cut two stockings, reversing one.

Assembly

Sew seams with right sides together using a ¼-inch seam allowance unless otherwise noted.

1. Fuse stripe toes to two opposite-facing stockings cut from Christmas print fabric.

2. Fuse interfacing to the wrong side of each stocking piece to which a toe was adhered. Sew stocking pieces together, leaving upper edges open; turn right side out and press.

3. Sew remaining stocking pieces together for lining, leaving upper edges open. Place lining inside the stocking, matching side seams and upper edges. Baste upper edges of stocking and lining together.

4. Sew two cuff pieces together at both side seams; repeat with remaining cuff pieces and turn right side out. With right sides together and raw edges even, matching side seams, sew both sets of cuffs together along zigzag edge. Clip corners and trim points. Turn right side out. Press.

5. Place the cuff around the top of the stocking with the side seams matching and the upper edges even. Cut a 6-inch strip of bias trim and fold in half to make a loop. Edgestitch along long edge. Baste the loop inside the stocking at the back seam, with the cut edges even (Figure 6).

Figure 6

6. Wrap bias trim over the top edges of the stocking and cuff, and edgestitch in place (Figure 7a). Fold the hanging loop up and stitch to secure (Figure 7b).

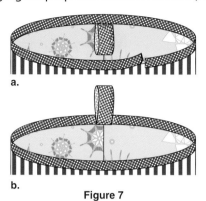

a.

b.

Figure 7

7. Edgestitch a length of bias trim around end of toe. Sew header of beaded trim to zigzag edge of cuff. Glue red gimp trim over seam line at toe and along zigzag edge of cuff. ❖

Sources: *Cotton fabrics and bias trim from Michael Miller Fabrics; ribbon from May Arts; beaded trim, gimp trim and tassels from Expo International; Fabri-Tac permanent fabric adhesive from Beacon Adhesives.*

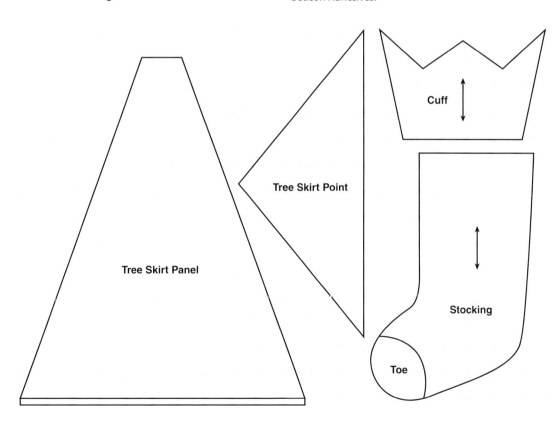

Whimsical Tree Skirt & Stocking
Templates
1 square = 1"

Elegant Stripes
Mantel Cloth & Pillow

Mix and match strips of elegant fabrics to create beautiful decorating accents that will add instant holiday glamour to any decor.

Mantel Cloth

Finished Size
18 x 72 inches

Materials
- ¼ yard each assorted decorator fabrics
- 2⅛ yards taffeta for backing
- 3½ yards beaded trim with decorative header
- Basic sewing supplies and equipment

Note: *To adjust mantel cloth size, plan a cloth that is 12 inches longer than your mantel length and 6 inches deeper than your mantel depth. Increase or decrease the template on page 24 by spreading or folding the enlarged template by the difference in the template and your mantel measurements. Yardages below are for sample size of 18 x 72 inches. Adjust fabric measurements accordingly.*

Tips & Techniques

Anytime you are sewing strips of fabric together to create your own decorative fabric, choose fabrics of similar weights and complementary colors. We chose taffeta, lightweight velvet, velveteen, silk and embroidered taffeta for these projects. If you have a sewing machine that embroiders, you could add an even more personal touch by embroidering designs of your choosing on any of the strips.

Cutting
- Cut fabric remnants into 19-inch-long strips, ranging in width from 2 inches to 5 inches.

Assembly
Sew seams with right sides together using a ¼-inch seam allowance unless otherwise noted.

1. Sew long edges of strips together, varying widths, colors and textures, to a length of approximately 38 inches.

2. Enlarge mantel cloth template as indicated; use template with pattern tracing cloth or paper to make a pattern. Use pattern to cut mantel cloth top from pieced strips and mantel cloth back from taffeta.

3. Sew top to back, leaving a 10-inch opening along straight edge. Turn right side out and press. Slipstitch opening closed. Sew decorative trim header along side and front edges.

Pillow

Finished Size
16 x 16 inches

Materials
- Assorted remnants decorator fabric
- ⅔ yard velveteen
- 16 x 16-inch pillow form
- 2 yards beaded trim with decorative header
- Basic sewing supplies and equipment

Cutting
From decorator fabrics:
- Cut 18-inch-long strips ranging from 1½ inches to 3 inches wide for pillow front.

From velveteen:
- Cut one 17 x 17-inch square for pillow back.
- Cut 3 strips each 18 inches long, ranging from 1½ inches to 3 inches wide for pillow front.

Assembly

Sew seams with right sides together using a ¼-inch seam allowance unless otherwise noted.

1. Sew long edges of strips together, varying the widths, colors and textures, to form an 18-inch-wide panel. Press seams in one direction. Trim even to 17 inches square (Figure 1).

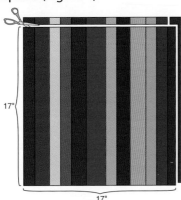

17"

17"

Figure 1

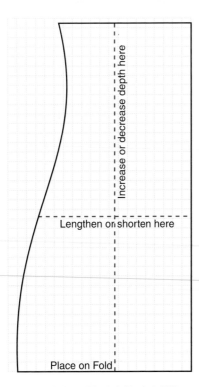

Increase or decrease depth here

Lengthen or shorten here

Place on Fold

Elegant Stripes Mantel Cloth & Pillow
Templates
1 square = 1"

2. Sew pieced front to velveteen back, leaving an 8-inch opening in center of one side. Turn right side out and press.

3. Insert pillow form. Slipstitch opening closed.

4. Position decorative trim header just above seam and glue around edge of pillow (Figure 2). ❖

Figure 2

Sources: *Fabrics from Bonavista Fabrics and RJR Fabrics; trim from Expo International; Fabri-Tac permanent fabric adhesive from Beacon Adhesives.*

Richly Jeweled Runner

Beautiful decorator fabrics and trims combine to create a touch of elegance for your holiday table with this pieced runner.

Finished Size
16 x 60 inches

Materials
- 54-inch-wide decorator fabrics:
    - ⅓ yard black/gold scroll print
    - ¼ yard red/gold velveteen fabric
    - ½ yard gold damask
- 1 yard 44/45-inch-wide silk fabric
- 1 yard ½-inch-wide gold gimp trim
- 1 yard black/gold beaded fringe with header
- 2 yards low-loft batting
- 2¾ yards ½-inch-wide black/gold flat bead trim
- 4 yards 2-inch-long gold tassel trim with decorative header
- Basting tape
- Permanent fabric adhesive
- Basic sewing supplies and equipment

Cutting

From black/gold scroll print:
- Cut one 11 x 31-inch rectangle for center panel (A).

From red velveteen:
- Cut two 4 x 31-inch strips for side borders (B).
- Cut two 4 x 17-inch strips for end borders (C).

From gold damask:
- Referring to Cutting Diagram on page 26, cut two end panels (D).

From gold silk:
- Cut two 17 x 32-inch rectangles for backing.

From low-loft batting:
- Cut one 17 x 62-inch rectangle.

From gold gimp:
- Cut two 17-inch lengths.

From beaded fringe with header:
- Cut two 17-inch lengths.

From flat bead trim:
- Cut two 30-inch and two 17-inch lengths.

Assembly
Sew right sides together using a ½-inch seam allowance unless otherwise noted.

1. Referring to Assembly Diagram, sew side border strips (B) to long edges of center panel (A). Press seam allowances toward borders. Sew end border strips (C) to each ends of pieced unit. Press seams toward borders. Sew end panels (D) to end borders (C). Press seams open.

Richly Jeweled Runner
Assembly Diagram

2. Baste header of beaded fringe to wrong side of gimp using basting tape. Repeat for each length. Apply basted gimp/fringe centered over seams of end triangles (Figure 1). Sew in place.

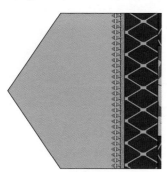

Figure 1

3. Sew short edges of two backing rectangles together, leaving an 8-inch opening at center of seam. Place backing piece right side up on batting; place runner top right sides together with backing piece, aligning long edges. Pin layers together, keeping beaded trim away from stitching area. Trim batting and backing to match runner top.

4. Sew all layers together. Trim points and turn right side out through opening in backing. Press. Slipstitch opening closed.

5. Glue flat bead trim over top, bottom and side seams of center panel (Figure 2).

Figure 2

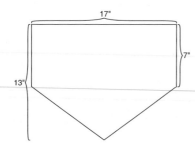

Richly Jeweled Runner
End Panel Cutting Diagram

6. Pin tassel trim to outside edges of runner; stitch at top and bottom of trim (Figure 3). ❖

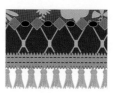

Figure 3

Sources: *Decorator fabrics from Waverly Fabrics; silk fabric from RJR Fabrics; beaded fringe, flat bead trim, gimp trim and tassel trim from Expo International; Poly-fil low-loft batting from Fairfield Processing; Fabri-Tac permanent fabric adhesive from Beacon Adhesives.*

Pressing Tips

Decorator fabrics often require special handling when pressing. Here are a few tips to remember:

1. Always have press cloths, pressing hams and sleeve rolls on hand. Use a well-padded ironing board.

2. Wool: Use hot steam. Always use a press cloth and usually press on the wrong side.

3. Rayon/silk: Always press on the wrong side using a warm iron and light steam.

4. Synthetics: Test iron heat on fabric scrap. Some synthetics will melt and do not care for steam.

5. Cotton: Can be pressed from either side with or without hot steam.

6. Linen: Can be pressed from either side with or without hot steam.

7. Embroidered fabrics: Press from the wrong side over a plush white towel, with or without steam.

8. Velvet/velveteen: Press from the wrong side over a plush white towel or needle board (a board with metal brush-like tips). Hold iron above the fabric using medium heat and steam.

Fun & Festive Table Ensemble

Perky fabrics with a retro look add fun and whimsy to this festive holiday table ensemble.

Table Runner

Finished Size
13 x 53 inches

Materials
- 44/45-inch-wide cotton fabrics:
    - ¼ yard large print
    - 1 yard medium print
    - ⅛ yard each dark green and light green small print
- 2 (9 x 18-inch) fusible web sheets
- 4⅞ yards ⅜-inch-wide green patterned ribbon
- ¼-inch-wide fusible web tape
- 12-weight green cotton thread
- Two 5-inch-long red tassels
- Basic sewing supplies and equipment

Cutting
Note: Save any remnants for assembly of place mats, tea cozy and napkin rings.

From large print:
- Cut one 7 x 44-inch rectangle for center panel (A).

From medium print:
- Cut two 4½ x 44-inch strips for borders (B).
- Cut two 14 x 28-inch rectangles for backing.
- Use template on page 32 to cut two end panels (C).

From dark green and light green small print:
- Using holly leaf template on page 32, trace 14 holly leaves onto paper backing of fusible web, spacing at least ½ inch apart. Cut out slightly outside traced lines. Fuse seven holly leaves each to wrong sides of light green and dark green small print fabric. Cut out leaves on traced lines. Remove paper backing. Set aside.

From ribbon:
- Cut two 44-inch lengths.
- Cut two 14-inch lengths.

Assembly
Sew seams with right sides together using ½-inch seam allowance.

1. Sew border strips (B) to center panel (A). Press seams toward borders. Center and fuse 44-inch length ribbon lengths over seams using fusible web tape. Stitch in place along both ribbon edges using 12-weight thread. Sew end panel (C) to each end of A/B unit (Figure 1). Press seams toward center panel.

Figure 1

2. Referring to Figure 2, arrange seven leaves on each border, alternating colors. Fuse in place.

Figure 2

3. Use 12-weight thread to topstitch a curving line down the border strip through centers of leaves. Stitch edges of each leaf with 12-weight thread and medium-width zigzag (Figure 3).

Figure 3

4. Center and fuse two 14-inch lengths of ribbon over end-panel seams. Stitch along ribbon edges. Trim ribbon ends even with table runner edges.

5. Sew short edges of backing rectangles together, leaving 6-inch opening in center of seam. Press seam open. Pin runner top to back, right sides together. Trim back to match top.

6. Slip tassel loops between points of end panels with tassels toward center of runner (Figure 4).

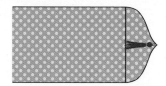

Figure 4

7. Sew front and back together. Turn right side out through opening in back seam. Press. Slipstitch opening closed.

Tea Cozy

Finished Size
13 x 13 inches

Materials
- 44/45-inch-wide cotton fabric:
    - ⅓ yard large print
    - ⅝ yard medium print
- Remnants light green and dark green small print from Table Runner
- 9 x 18-inch sheet fusible web
- Insul-Bright insulating batting
- ⅞ yard ⅜-inch-wide green patterned ribbon
- ¼-inch-wide fusible web tape
- 3-inch red tassel
- Basic sewing supplies and equipment

Cutting

From large print:
- Cut two 10 x 14-inch rectangles for top.

From medium print:
- Cut two 4½ x 14-inch strips for borders.
- Cut two 14 x 14-inch squares for lining.

From dark green and light green small print:
- Using holly leaf template on page 32, trace four holly leaves onto paper backing of fusible web, spacing ¼ inch apart. Cut out slightly outside traced lines. Fuse two holly leaves each onto wrong sides of light green and dark green small print fabric. Cut out leaves on traced lines. Remove paper backing. Set aside.

From insulating batting:
- Cut two 14 x 14-inch squares.

From ribbon:
- Cut two 15-inch lengths.

Assembly
Sew seams with right sides together using a ¼-inch seam allowance unless otherwise noted.

1. Sew one border strip to 14-inch edge of top, matching raw edges. Press seams toward border. Repeat with second border and top.

2. Use fusible web tape to fuse a 15-inch length of ribbon over each border/ top seam. Stitch along both edges of ribbon. Trim ribbon ends even with border/top.

3. Referring to Figure 5, fold each border/top piece in half. Cut rounded upper corners using a dinner plate or similar object as

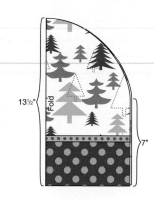

13½" |Fold   7"

Figure 5

a template, then open the shaped piece and use it as a template to trim the corners of the remaining border/top piece, the batting and the lining pieces.

4. Fuse two holly leaves to each border strip. Stitch a curved line across border and through leaves, and zigzag leaf edges as in step 3 of Table Runner.

5. Adhere batting pieces to wrong sides of appliquéd top/bottom pieces using temporary spray adhesive. Attach tassel to right side of center top of one appliquéd piece. Sew appliquéd pieces together, leaving bottom edges open. Turn right side out.

6. Sew lining sides together, leaving a 6-inch opening in seam. Do not turn.

7. Slip lining over appliquéd piece so right sides are facing each other. Sew bottom edges together. Turn right side out through opening in lining. Slipstitch opening closed and insert lining in place. Press. Topstitch ¼ inch from bottom edge.

Place Mat

Finished Size
Place Mat: 14 x 18 inches

Materials for Two
- 1 yard 44-inch-wide medium- to heavyweight red cotton fabric
- Remnants light green and dark green small print cotton fabric from Table Runner
- 9 x 18-inch sheet fusible web
- 28 inches ⅜-inch-wide green patterned ribbon
- ¼-inch-wide fusible web tape
- 4 yards 1-inch-wide white pin-dot double-fold bias trim
- 12-weight cotton thread
- Basic sewing supplies and equipment

Cutting
From red fabric:
- Cut four 14 x 18-inch rectangles for top and bottom.

From dark green and light green small print:
- Using holly leaf template on page 32, trace six holly leaves onto paper backing of fusible web, spacing ¼ inch apart. Cut out slightly outside traced lines. Fuse three holly leaves each onto wrong sides of light green and dark green small print fabric. Cut out leaves on traced lines. Remove paper backing. Set aside.

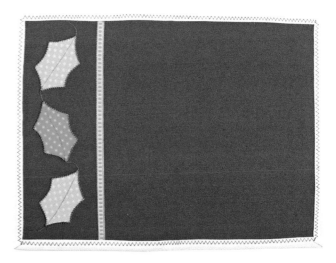

Assembly
1. Using photo as a guide, fuse leaves to left sides of two place mat fronts alternating colors, approximately 1½ inches from edge.

2. Use fusible web tape to fuse a 14-inch length of ribbon approximately 5 inches from the left edge (Figure 6). Stitch along both edges of ribbon.

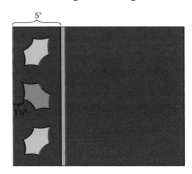

Figure 6

3. Stitch a curving line through leaves and zigzag leaf edges as in step 3 of Table Runner.

4. Layer rectangles wrong sides together. Zigzag-stitch edges together. Wrap bias trim over edges and zigzag-stitch in place using a wide stitch and 12-weight thread.

Napkin Ring

Finished Size
5½ x 2½ inches

Materials for Two
- Remnants green small print fabric from Table Runner
- Low-loft cotton batting

- 2 (12-inch) lengths ⅜-inch-wide green patterned ribbon
- 2 (1-inch) red buttons
- Basic sewing supplies and equipment

Cutting

From green small print:
- Using holly leaf template, trace eight holly leaves onto wrong sides of fabric remnants, spacing at least ½ inch apart. Cut out ¼ inch beyond traced lines.

From low-loft cotton batting:
- Using same holly leaf template, trace two holly leaves onto batting. Cut out on traced lines.

Assembly

Sew right sides together using a ¼-inch seam allowance unless otherwise noted.

1. Sew pairs of leaves right sides together, leaving an opening at the base of each leaf. Turn right side out and press.

2. Insert a batting leaf into each fabric leaf and slip-stitch opening closed.

3. Topstitch around leaf edges and through centers.

4. Using photo as a guide, overlap two leaves at base and tack together. Sew a button over joining.

5. Center 12-inch length of ribbon on back of joining and tack in place. To use, tie ribbon around napkin. ❖

Sources: *Fabric and bias trim from Michael Miller Fabrics; Steam-A-Seam 2 fusible web sheets, fusible web tape and Insul-Bright insulating batting from The Warm Company; ribbon from May Arts; 12-weight cotton thread from Sulky of America; tassels from Expo International.*

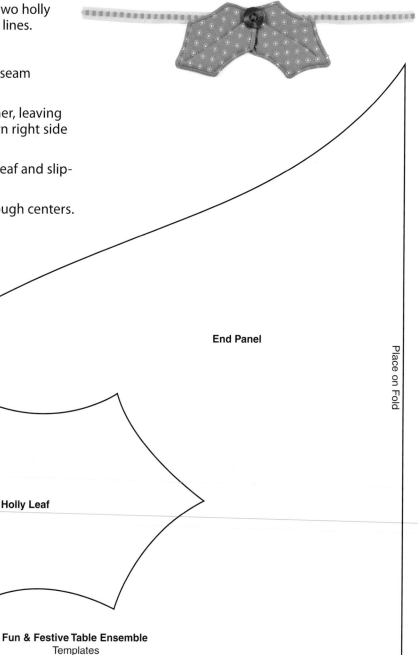

End Panel

Place on Fold

Holly Leaf

Fun & Festive Table Ensemble
Templates

Friendly Santa Coasters

Let jolly old Saint Nick protect your table tops when you make these fun-to-piece Santa coasters.

Finished Size
5 x 5 inches

Materials for a Set of Four
- 44/45-inch-wide cotton fabrics:
    - ¼ yard red print
    - ¼ yard white print
    - ¼ yard solid pink
- ¼ yard needled cotton batting
- Scraps felt:
    - black for eyes
    - pink for nose
    - red for mouth
- ⅔ yard ½-inch-wide white gimp
- 12-weight white cotton thread
- ⅛ yard paper-backed fusible web
- 4 small white pompoms
- Permanent fabric adhesive
- Clear ruler
- Basic sewing supplies and equipment

Cutting
From red print:
- Cut four 3 x 8½-inch strips.
- Cut four 5½ x 5½-inch squares for backs.

From white print:
- Cut four 4½ x 8½-inch strips.

From solid pink:
- Cut four 1¾ x 8½-inch strips.

From cotton batting:
- Cut four 5½ x 5½-inch squares.

From scraps black, red and pink felt:
- Using templates on page 34, trace four of each eye, four noses and four mouths onto paper backing of fusible web, spacing ¼-inch apart. Cut out slightly outside traced lines. Fuse pieces to appropriate felt colors and cut out on traced lines. Remove paper backing; set aside.

From gimp trim:
- Cut four 6-inch lengths.

Assembly
Sew right sides together, using a ¼-inch seam allowance unless otherwise noted.

1. Sew a red print strip to a pink strip. Sew a white print strip to opposite edge of pink strip (Figure 1). Press seams in same direction. Repeat to create four coaster fronts.

Figure 1

2. Using clear ruler and rotary cutter, cut each front to 5½ x 5½ inches, with top edge of white strip centered vertically between top and bottom points of square so the seam intersects the side corners perfectly (Figure 2).

Figure 2

4. Center gimp over pink/red print seam. Stitch in place, along both edges. Trim ends even. Repeat for each coaster.

5. Remove paper backing from felt pieces. Fuse two eyes, one nose and one mouth onto each pieced

front, referring to photo for placement. Edgestitch each piece in place using matching thread. Use 12-weight white cotton thread to straight-stitch a mustache line from below nose to top of white fabric, beginning and ending stitching ¼ inch from each side (Figure 3).

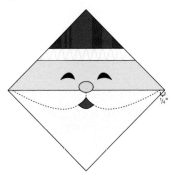

Figure 3

6. For each coaster, layer front and back, right sides together, on a 5½ x 5½-inch piece of batting. Sew around the edges, leaving an opening for turning. Turn right side out; press and slipstitch openings closed.

7. Glue one small white pompom to the point of each coaster. ❖

Sources: *Needled cotton batting from Fairfield Processing; Steam-A-Seam 2 fusible web from The Warm Company.*

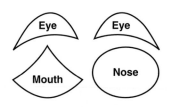

Santa Coasters
Templates
Actual Size

Dress Up Your Table

Stitch up this easy tablecloth in no time to create a festive table for your holiday guests.

Finished Size
60 x 84 inches

Materials
• 44/45-inch-wide cotton print fabrics:
    2 yards holiday
    1 yard each three coordinating
• Basic sewing supplies and equipment

Cutting
From holiday print:
• Cut one 44 x 68-inch rectangle for tablecloth center.

From each of three coordinating prints:
• Cut 17 (2-inch-wide) strips across the width of the fabric.

Assembly
Sew seams right sides together using ¼-inch seam allowance unless otherwise noted.

1. Sew long edges of 2-inch-wide strips together in groups of three repeating the same sequence (Figure 1). Press seam allowances in one direction.

Figure 1

2. With strips running horizontally, cut through the panel vertically to make four 10-inch-long sections (Figure 2).

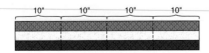

Figure 2

3. Sew the sections together to make one continuous border strip as shown in Figure 3.

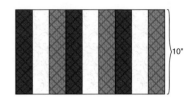

Figure 3

4. From the border strip, cut two 65-inch-long end borders and two 89-inch-long side borders. Match the centers of borders to sides and ends of tablecloth center. Pin borders in place.

5. Sew the borders to tablecloth center, mitering corners (Figure 4). ***Note:*** *See Mitering Borders on page 60.* Trim corners. Press seams toward center.

Figure 4

6. Press under raw edge of borders in a double ½-inch hem. ***Note:*** *See Mitering Double-Fold Hems on page 61.* Topstitch hem in place. ❖

Source: *Fabric from Michael Miller Fabrics.*

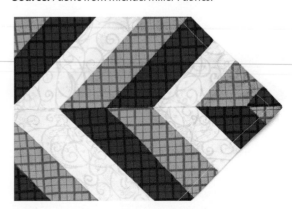

Polka Dots & Stripes Table Set

Ribbon-trimmed place mats with stockings to hold your silverware are a great way to bring a holiday spark to any meal during the season.

Finished Sizes
Place Mat: 13 x 18 inches
Silverware Stocking: 6½ x 5 inches

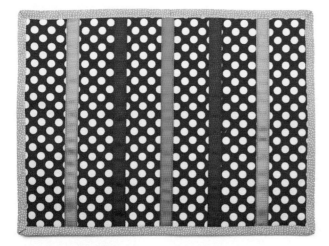

Place Mats

Materials for Two
- 1 yard 44/45-inch-wide red polka-dot cotton fabric
- 3½ yards green pin-dot bias binding
- ¾-inch-wide grosgrain ribbon:
    1⅜ yards each red and light green
    ⅞ yard dark green
- Low-loft batting
- Basic sewing supplies and equipment

Cutting
From polka-dot fabric:
- Cut four 13 x 18-inch rectangles for place mat front and backs.

From batting:
- Cut two 13 x 18-inch rectangles.

From grosgrain ribbons:
- Cut four 13-inch lengths red.
- Cut four 13-inch lengths light green.
- Cut two 13-inch lengths dark green.

Note: Reserve excess ribbon for stockings.

Assembly
Follow instructions for each place mat.

1. Pin dark green ribbon centered on right side of place mat front. Pin red and light green ribbons 2⅛ inches apart on either side of dark green ribbon. Edgestitch ribbons in place (Figure 1).

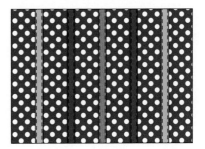

Figure 1

2. Sandwich batting between place mat front and back. Zigzag-stitch edges.

3. Beginning in center of one long edge, wrap bias binding over place mat edge, cutting end 1 inch past beginning. Fold raw edge to wrong side and overlap beginning raw edge. Edgestitch binding in place.

Stocking Silverware Holders

Materials for Two
- 9 x 12-inch rectangle each white, green and red wool felt
- Small ball fringe with header:
    ¼ yard red
    ¼ yard white
- Ribbon scraps from place mats
- Basic sewing supplies and equipment

Cutting

From white wool felt:
- Use template to cut one stocking for front.
- Cut three circles, ranging from 1 to 1½ inches diameter.

From green wool felt:
- Use template to cut one stocking for front.
- Use templates to cut one each cuff, heel and toe.

From red wool felt:
- Use templates to cut one each cuff, heel and toe.

Assembly

1. Pin white wool circles to green stocking front Edgestitch in place.

2. Cut ribbon scraps to fit diagonally across front of white stocking front, spacing ⅜ inch apart. Edgestitch in place.

3. Using photo as a guide, pin heel and toe pieces to stocking fronts, aligning edges, and edgestitch along inner edges (Figure 2).

Figure 2

4. Baste ball fringe across top of each stocking. Pin and then double-stitch cuffs over ball fringe header (Figure 3).

Figure 3

5. Using assembled fronts as templates, cut stocking backs from matching felt. Sew fronts and backs right sides together, using a ¼-inch seam allowance. Turn right side out through top opening; finger-press. ❖

Sources: *Fabric and bias binding from Michael Miller Fabrics; ribbon from May Arts; Poly-fil low-loft batting from Fairfield Processing; wool felt from National Nonwovens; ball fringe from Expo International.*

> ## *Tips & Techniques*
> *When trying to attach small pieces of trim or fabric to a project, pins can sometimes be cumbersome. Try using one of the many varieties of basting tapes available. It can be cut to an appropriate size to hold smaller pieces in place, and machines will sew over it with no problems!*

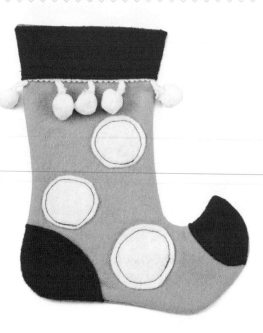

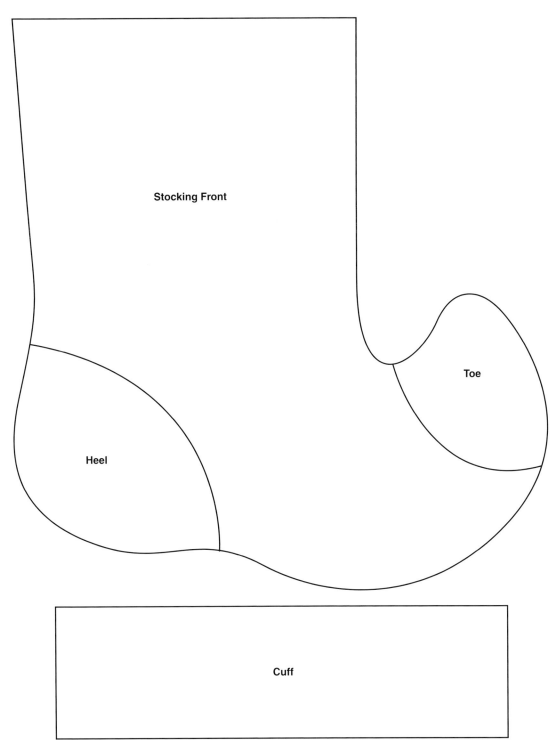

Stocking Front

Toe

Heel

Cuff

Polka Dots & Stripes Table Set
Templates
Actual Size

House of White Birches, Berne, Indiana 46711   DRGnetwork.com

Christmas Casserole Caddies

Serve holiday meals in style with quilted casserole caddies that are perfect for taking hot dishes to all your holiday parties.

Finished Sizes
Round: 15 inches in diameter (fits 9-inch-diameter casserole dish)
Square: 15 x 15 inches (fits 9 x 9-inch casserole dish)

Materials
- 44/45-inch-wide fabric:
  ½ yard reversible quilted
  ½ yard coordinating print
- Coordinating ribbon:
  2 yards 1-inch-wide
  1½ yards ⅜-inch-wide
- Optional: bias-tape maker to make 1-inch-wide double-fold bias tape
- Basic sewing supplies and equipment

Project Note
Materials listed will make one each round and square caddy.

Cutting
From quilted fabric:
- Cut one 15 x 15-inch square.
- Cut one 15-inch-diameter circle.

From coordinating print fabric:
Note: Follow instructions with bias-tape maker, or refer to Making Bias Tape on page 44.

- Cut bias strips and make 1¾ yards 1-inch-wide double-fold bias tape for square caddy and 1½ yards for round caddy.

From 1-inch-wide coordinating ribbon:
- Cut four 18-inch lengths.

Assembly
1. Zigzag-stitch edges of quilted pieces. Bind zigzagged edges by covering with bias tape and edgestitching in place. End binding by cutting 1 inch past beginning; turn cut end to wrong side, then overlap beginning end and finish stitching.

2. Mark a 2½ x 2½-inch square at each corner of the quilted square. Mark 1-inch buttonholes as shown in Figure 1. Stitch buttonholes.

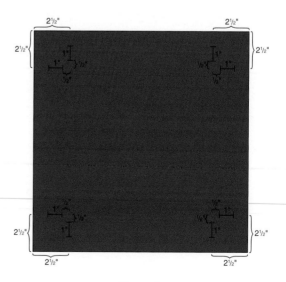

Figure 1

Tips & Techniques
Changing the sizes of these caddies to fit your casserole dishes is a snap. Measure the bottom of the dish, add the depth of the sides plus ½ inch to each side for overall length and width.

Example, for a 13 x 9 inch casserole dish:
Length: 13 + 2 + ½ = 15½ inches
Width: 9 + 2 + ½ = 11½ inches

3. Thread 18-inch ribbon lengths through buttonhole sets in each corner of square caddy. Place casserole dish inside caddy and tie ends of each ribbon together, pulling on corners of caddy to adjust fit.

4. Mark and stitch buttonholes on round quilted piece ¾ inch from outer bound edge (Figure 2).

5. Weave ⅜-inch-wide ribbon through buttonholes in round caddy. Set round casserole dish in caddy and pull ribbon edges evenly to fit. ❖

Sources: *Fabric from Fabri-Quilt Inc.; ribbon from May Arts; Bias tape maker from Clover Needlecraft.*

Figure 2

Making Bias Tape

Determining Amount
• A 12 x 12-inch square of fabric will yield 144 inches of 1-inch-wide bias strips or 72 inches of 2-inch-wide bias strips. Multiply the width by length of a fabric square and divide by the width of the bias strip that is to be cut to find the total length of bias that can be made.

• Determine the width of bias strip needed for your project using the formulas below.

Double-Fold Bias Tape

Width of finished tape x 4 = width of bias strip to cut. *Example: ½ inch x 4 = 2 inches.*

Single-Fold Bias Tape

Width of finished tape x 2 = width of bias strip to cut. *Example: ½ inch x 2 = 1 inch.*

Cutting Bias Strips
• Fold fabric diagonally so crosswise grain straight edge is parallel to selvage or lengthwise grain. Cut fabric along this fold line to mark the true bias (Figure 1).

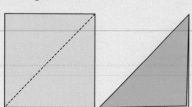

Figure 1

• Using a clear ruler, mark successive bias lines the width of bias strip desired. Carefully cut

along line. Handle edges carefully to avoid stretching (Figure 2).

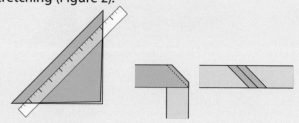

Figure 2   Figure 3

Preparing Double-Fold Bias
• Position and pin individual bias strips perpendicular to each other with raw edges aligned and right sides together. Sew a diagonal seam to join in a continuous strip. Trim seams to ¼ inch and press open (Figure 3).

• Fold strip in half, wrong sides together. Press.

• Open out with wrong side up. Fold each edge to center fold and press. Fold in half again and press (Figure 4).

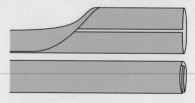

Figure 4

Preparing Single-Fold Bias
• Fold bias strips in half, wrong sides together. Press.

• Open out with wrong side up. Fold each edge to center and press (Figure 5).

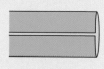

Figure 5

Ribbon & Ornament Tea Towels

Dressed up with ribbon and ball fringe, these appliquéd towels are perfect for adding a colorful accent to your kitchen or for giving as a gift.

Finished Size
16 x 26 inches

Materials for One Towel
- 44/45-inch-wide cotton fabric
  - ½ yard mediumweight white
  - ⅜ yard print
- Scrap each four coordinating prints
- One 9 x 12-inch red felt square
- 1 yard each 3 ribbons ranging in widths from ⅛ to ⅜ inches
- ½ yard small ball fringe with header
- 9 x 12-inch sheet paper-backed fusible web
- ¼-inch-wide fusible web tape
- Basic sewing supplies and equipment

Cutting
From mediumweight white cotton fabric:
- Cut one 17 x 22-inch rectangle for towel body.

From cotton print:
- Cut one 17 x 9-inch rectangle for towel border.

From felt square:
- Cut four ½ x 1-inch rectangles for ornament toppers.

From ribbon:
- Cut each ribbon into one 12-inch and one 24-inch length.

Appliqué Preparation
1. Trace ornament templates (page 46) onto paper side of fusible web sheet. Cut out slightly beyond traced line.

2. Following manufacturer's instructions, fuse each ornament to wrong side of a different coordinating print. Cut out on traced lines.

3. Remove paper backing. Set aside.

Assembly
1. Press cotton print border in half lengthwise, wrong sides together. Baste raw edges together. Sew border strip to the right side of one 17-inch edge of the towel body. Press seam toward border (Figure 1).

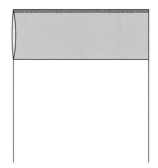

Figure 1

2. Press side edges of towel and border under in a doubled ¼-inch hem; edgestitch in place. Repeat for top edge of towel (Figure 2).

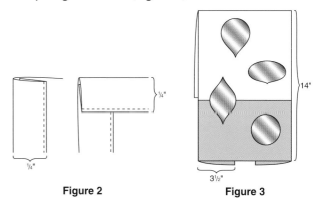

Figure 2　　　　　Figure 3

4. Fold 3½ inches on long edges of towel to wrong side; press. Fold towel crosswise so front is approximately 14 inches long. Arrange ornaments on front of towel as desired and fuse in place (Figure 3).

House of White Birches, Berne, Indiana 46711　DRGnetwork.com

5. Satin-stitch over edges of each ornament. Place a felt rectangle at top of each ornament and edgestitch (Figure 4).

Figure 4

6. Apply ¼-inch-wide fusible web tape to wrong side of each 24-inch length of ribbon. Trim web tape width to ribbon width. Position ribbons from tops of ornaments to top of towel. Ribbon should extend ½ inch beyond top of towel. Wrap ribbon end to back of towel and fuse ribbon length to towel. Edgestitch along both edges of ribbon (Figure 5).

7. Using 12-inch lengths of ribbon, tie a bow and hand-stitch to tops of ornaments.

8. Pin and stitch bottom edge of towel border over top of ball-fringe header. ❖

Sources: *Fabric from Michael Miller Fabrics; ribbon from May Arts; ball fringe from Expo International; Steam-A-Seam 2 fusible web sheets and tape from The Warm Company.*

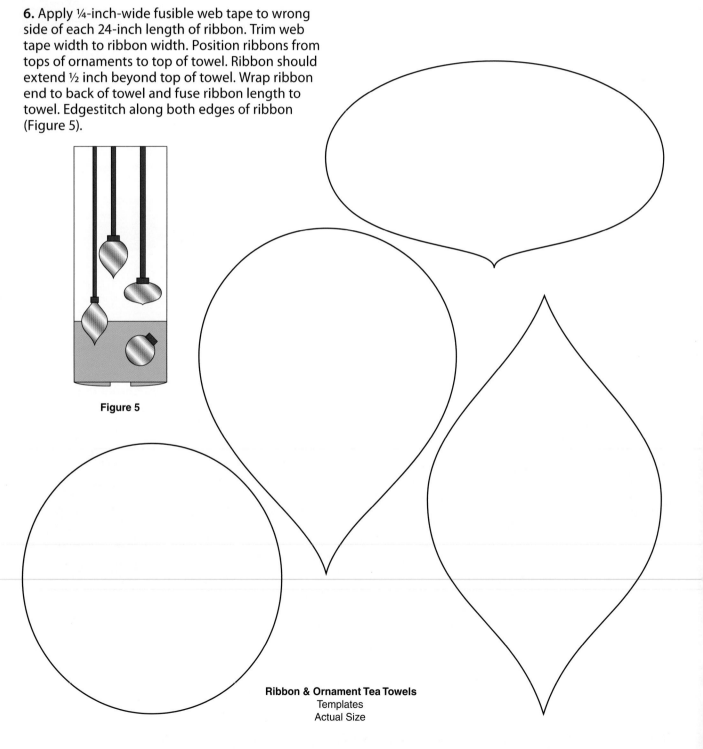

Figure 5

Ribbon & Ornament Tea Towels
Templates
Actual Size

Embossed Velvet Gift Bag

The easy technique of embossing velvet using a rubber stamp adds a special touch to a handmade wine or gift bag.

Finished Size
5½ x 14 inches

Materials
- ⅝ yard rayon lightweight velvet fabric
- ¼ yard silver lamé fabric
- 2 inches 1-inch-wide silver metallic ribbon
- 18 inches pearl-bead strand, narrow ribbon or cord
- 12 x 12-inch square low-loft batting
- Rubber stamp (see How to Emboss Velvet)
- Spray bottle of water
- Basting tape
- Basic sewing supplies and equipment

Cutting
From lightweight velvet:
- Cut one 12 x 12-inch piece for outer bag. Emboss, following instruction below.

How to Emboss Velvet
- Select a rubber stamp with a simple design and deep cuts.
- Preheat a dry iron to medium-hot. Place rubber stamp stamp-side up on a heat-resistant surface.
- Place the velvet right side down on top of the stamp. Lightly mist the wrong side of the velvet with water.
- Press the iron straight down on the velvet-topped stamp. Hold the iron firmly in place for 20 to 30 seconds and lift straight up without sliding the iron.
- Remove the velvet from the stamp.
- Repeat to emboss the velvet in a random pattern with as many images as desired.

Tips & Techniques
Want to add even more glamour to this elegant wine bag? Attach tassels or assorted glass beads to the ends of the pearl-bead string, ribbon or cord!

From silver lamé:
- Cut one 7 x 12-inch rectangle for upper band.

Assembly
Use a ½-inch seam allowance unless otherwise noted.

1. Adhere batting to wrong side of outer bag piece, using temporary spray adhesive.

2. Fold the metallic ribbon in half and adhere the cut edges together with basting tape. Fold the outer bag piece in half, wrong sides together. Mark the center top edge of one side (this will be the back). Use basting tape to adhere the ribbon loop over the center mark, aligning the cut edges of the ribbon with the raw edge of the fabric. Unfold bag.

3. Use a press cloth to press the lamé strip in half lengthwise with wrong sides together. Adhere the long raw edges together with basting tape. With raw edges even, sew the folded lamé strip to the right side of the bag. Finger-press the seam allowance toward the lamé upper band.

4. Fold the bag in half with right sides together and the band at the top. Sew the side and bottom edges together. Trim corners and turn right side out.

5. Insert the pearl-bead string, narrow ribbon or cord through the ribbon loop on the back of the bag. Insert wine bottle into the bag and tie the pearl-bead string, ribbon or cord around the neck. ❖

Source: *Wonder Tape basting tape from Prym Consumer USA.*

Sew a Wallet

Looking for the perfect gift? Make this quilted wallet that doubles as a handbag when you add the removable strap. The inside features a zippered coin compartment and plenty of pockets.

Finished Size
9 x 4 inches, excluding strap

Materials
- ⅓ yard reversible quilted fabric
- 44-inch-wide lightweight woven fabric:
  ½ yard stripe
  1 yard print
- ½ yard fusible interfacing
- 2 (1-inch) swivel spring clips for purse strap
- Magnetic snap with reinforcement plates, or large snap set
- 7-inch zipper
- 1½-inch button
- ½-inch-wide paper-backed fusible web tape
- 1-inch-wide double-fold bias-tape maker
- Basic sewing supplies and equipment

Cutting
From reversible quilted fabric:
- Cut one 9 x 11-inch rectangle for wallet body.

From stripe fabric:
- Cut two 7 x 9-inch rectangles for coin compartment.
- Cut one 4 x 8-inch rectangle for bottom pocket.
- Cut one 5 x 8-inch rectangle for large divided pocket.
- Cut one 3½ x 8-inch rectangle for small divided pocket.

From print fabric:
- Cut one 2 x 36-inch strip for strap.
- Cut one 2 x 55-inch bias strip for binding and strap loops.

From fusible interfacing:
- Cut one each 4 x 8-inch, 5 x 8-inch and 3½ x 8-inch rectangles for pockets.

Assembly
1. Press each 7 x 9-inch rectangle in half lengthwise, wrong sides together, to form two 3½ x 9-inch rectangles. Baste the raw edges of each rectangle together. Mark center of each folded edge.

2. Baste folded edge of one rectangle along zipper so center mark on edge is at center of zipper, and fold is centered along the teeth. Sew the fabric rectangle to the zipper tape.

3. Repeat to sew the remaining folded rectangle to the opposite zipper tape with the folds meeting in the center of the zipper teeth. Zigzag-stitch the folded edges together at each end of the zipper tape (Figure 1).

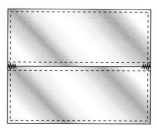

Figure 1

4. With the zipper at the top, fold the sides down and baste the lower edges together to make coin compartment (Figure 2).

Figure 2

5. Fuse interfacing to the wrong side of each pocket rectangle. On the right side of each pocket, apply fusible web tape along the top edge. Using the width of the tape as a guide, fold each edge under

twice; press. Unfold and remove the paper backing, then re-fold and fuse the edges in place. Topstitch ⅜ inch from each hemmed edge.

6. Place the 9 x 11-inch quilted rectangle on work surface with the inside fabric facing up. Layer the coin compartment, then the bottom pocket along the bottom edge of the rectangle, aligning the side and bottom edges. Baste the side and lower edges of the coin compartment/pocket to the quilted panel (Figure 3). Trim the top and bottom corners into curves through all layers.

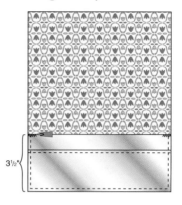

3½"

Figure 3

7. Press the 55-inch-long bias strip into double-folded bias binding. *Note: See Making Bias Tape on page 44.* Press the strip in half lengthwise with the raw edges on the inside.

8. Place the small pocket on top of the large pocket with the side and lower raw edges aligned. Baste the raw edges together. Cut a 9-inch strip of folded bias binding and wrap around the bottom edge. Stitch in place along the upper edge of the binding. Mark a stitching line at the vertical center of the pockets (Figure 4).

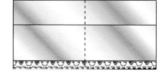

Figure 4

9. Pin the pockets to the quilted rectangle with the lower edge ½ inch above the coin compartment. Baste the side edges in place. Sew the bottom of the pocket in place close to the lower edge of the bias binding. Sew along the vertical center of the pockets, stitching through all layers (Figure 5).

Tips & Techniques

Constantly sliding items in and out of wallet pockets causes them to be the first to wear. Adding fusible web to the pocket hems of this wallet adds extra stability and longevity.

Simple objects can be used as templates to make rounded corners look even. Use a small bottle or salt shaker for small projects like this wallet. Lids, saucers and plates work well for larger curves.

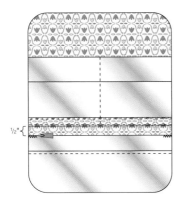

Figure 5

10. Cut two 3-inch bias binding strips. Edgestitch the folded edges of each strip together. Fold each strip in half to make a loop. On each side of the divided pockets, place a loop at the top edge with the raw edges even and baste in place (Figure 6).

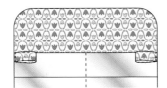

Figure 6

11. Beginning at the bottom of the quilted rectangle, wrap the bias binding around the edge and sew in place around the rectangle to within approximately 2 inches. Trim the binding 1 inch beyond the beginning end, fold ½ inch to the inside of the bias binding end and continue sewing in place.

12. Apply fusible web tape to the wrong side of the strap along both long edges. Press the edges to meet in the center, using the paper backing as a guide. Remove the backing and fuse the edges in place.

13. Fold the strap in half lengthwise, then press and edgestitch the folded edges together. Wrap each end of the strap through the loop of a spring clip and zigzag-stitch the end to the strap. Attach the clips to the loops on each side of the wallet.

14. Overlap the bottom third of the wallet with the top third. Mark the placement for each half of the snap at the center of the overlapping sections. Apply the snap halves. Sew the 1½-inch decorative button over the snap placement on the right side of the top overlap. ❖

Sources: *Fabric from Fabri-Quilt; Steam-A-Seam 2 fusible web from The Warm Company; Bias Tape Maker from Clover Needlecraft Inc.*

Christmastime Sweatshirt Jacket

Transform a sweatshirt into a holiday jacket by dressing it up with a fabric band, lamé bias and faux suede winterberry leaf appliqués.

Finished Size
Your size

Materials
Note: Materials listed are for size small sweatshirt. Adjust amounts as needed for larger or smaller sizes.
- Purchased black sweatshirt
- ¼ yard 44/45-inch-wide red cotton holiday print fabric
- ⅛ yard green faux suede
- 1½ yards ½-inch-wide red gimp trim
- 2 (27-inch lengths) green ¼-inch-wide fusible bias tape
- ⅝ yard ⅞-inch-wide red grosgrain ribbon
- Gold metallic thread
- Basting tape
- Basic sewing supplies and equipment

Sweatshirt Preparation
1. Carefully remove ribbing from sweatshirt neckline, cuffs and hem, cutting along stitching line for a straight edge.

2. Fold sweatshirt in half and mark center front. Referring to Figure 1, cut front only from neckline to hem on marked center front.

Figure 1

Cutting
From red holiday print:
- Cut two 3¼-inch-wide strips the width of fabric for front accent bands.

From green faux suede:
- Use leaf template on page 58 to cut 13 leaves.

From red gimp trim:
- Cut two 27-inch lengths.

Assembly
Sew right sides together using a ½-inch seam allowance unless otherwise noted.

1. Referring to Figure 2, pin right side of accent band to wrong side of sweatshirt along center front opening. Trim band to match sweatshirt neckline and bottom edge, then sew bands to sweatshirt along center front and neckline. Turn band to front. Press and baste in place.

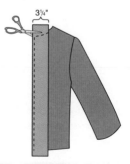

3¼"

Figure 2

2. Turn the raw edge of neckline between the two front bands ½ inch to the right side. Gently press and baste in place, taking care not to stretch neckline (Figure 3).

Figure 3

3. Cut a piece of ⅞-inch-wide red ribbon to fit neckline between front bands, adding 1 inch to length. Extending ribbon ends ½ inch under front bands, pin ribbon to right side of neckline, covering sweatshirt raw edge. Stitch close to both edges of ribbon (Figure 4).

Figure 4

4. Center and stitch a length of gimp trim over raw edge of each accent band. Referring to photo, arrange and fuse bias tape on each accent band for vine.

5. Arrange leaves along fusible bias vines, tacking base of each leaf in place with a small piece of basting tape. Using metallic thread in the needle and black thread in the bobbin, stitch a vein in the center of each leaf to attach to garment (Figure 5).

Figure 5

6. Turn up a 1-inch hem on sleeves and a ½-inch hem on bottom edge. Topstitch hems in place using metallic thread. ❖

Sources: *Sweatshirt from Fabric Café; fabric from Robert Kaufman Fabrics; Quick Bias green marble lamé stripe fusible bias tape from Clover Needlecraft Inc.; Holoshimmer gold metallic thread from Sulky of America; Collins Wonder Tape basting tape from Prym Consumer USA Inc.*

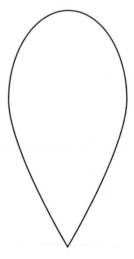

Christmastime Sweatshirt Jacket
Leaf Template
Actual Size

Here Comes Santa

Keep your favorite furry friend warm with a Santa coat, complete with a "HO HO" on the belt. A ribbon-trimmed leash and warm booties complete your pup's ensemble.

Finished Size
Custom

Materials
- Purchased pattern for lined pet coat with booties*
- 58/60-inch-wide fabric:
  red satin lining as indicated on pattern
    for contrast
  red plush as indicated on pattern
  black fleece as indicated on pattern,
    plus ⅛ yard for belt
  ½ yard white plush
  ¼ yard black faux suede for booties
  ⅛ yard black lining for belt
- Fusible mediumweight interfacing as indicated on pattern plus ⅛ yard for belt
- Elastic as indicated on pattern
- 1-inch-high iron-on velour letters
- 1½ yards ⅞-inch-wide red nylon webbing for leash
- Red novelty print ribbon:
    1½ yards of ⅝-inch-wide
    4 yards matching ⅜-inch-wide
- One package each white and black ½-inch-wide hook-and-loop tape
- ¼ yard ¼-inch-wide black ribbon
- 1 x 3-inch spring clasp for leash
- 35mm jingle bell
- Basic sewing supplies and equipment

*Sample project was completed using Kwik Sew pattern #2879, View A.

Cutting
From red satin lining:
- Use purchased pattern pieces to cut coat and collar.

Note: After cutting lining pieces for coat and collar, alter pattern pieces by drawing a line 1½ inches from side and bottom edges of coat pattern, and 1 inch from outer edge of collar pattern (Figure 1). Cut patterns along lines.

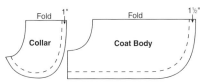

Figure 1

From red plush:
- Use altered pattern pieces to cut coat and collar, adding ¼-inch seam allowances (Figure 2a).

From black fleece:
- Use pattern pieces to cut booties.

From white plush:
- Use altered pattern pieces to cut coat and collar trim strips, adding ¼-inch seam allowances. (Figure 2b).

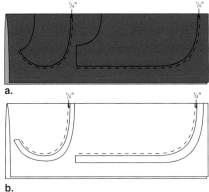

Figure 2

From black faux suede:
- Use pattern pieces to cut bootie contrast pieces.

Assembly
1. Sew white trim strips to coat and collar using ¼-inch seam allowances.

2. Follow pattern instructions to assemble coat, eliminating stomach strap.

3. Place coat on dog, fastening at neck. Determine placement of belt on coat and measure around dog. Add 4 inches to measurement for belt length.

4. From black fleece, black lining and interfacing, cut strips 2½ inches wide by belt length. Fuse interfacing to wrong side of fleece.

5. Sew fleece and lining wrong sides together using a ¼ inch seam, leaving an opening for turning. Turn right side out and slipstitch opening closed.

6. Follow manufacturer's instructions to fuse "HO HO" to center of belt, leaving 3 inches between words (Figure 3). Sew 35mm jingle bell between words. Tie an 18-inch strip of ⅜-inch-wide ribbon into a bow around bell. Sew hook-and-loop tape to belt, overlapping ends.

Figure 3

7. Place coat and belt on dog and fasten belt. Mark placement for two belt loops on back of coat. Remove coat and belt. Cut two 4-inch lengths of black ribbon and sew to coat at belt loop placement marks.

8. Following pattern instructions, apply suede toe and sole pieces to booties. Cut a strip of ⅜-inch-wide ribbon and center over seam of each suede piece (Figure 4). Edgestitch in place along both ribbon edges.

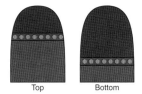

Top   Bottom

Figure 4

9. Cut eight 10-inch lengths of ⅜-inch-wide ribbon. Pin ends to bottom bootie piece, aligning them with stitched ribbon. Follow pattern instructions to assemble booties, being careful to catch only ends of ribbon in stitching.

10. Edgestitch ⅝-inch-wide ribbon down center of nylon webbing. Fold 7 inches of webbing to the back and securely sew ends in place for hand loop. Insert opposite end through ring on spring clamp and sew ends securely in place. ❖

Sources: *Pattern #2879 from Kwik Sew Pattern Co. Inc.; plush fabrics from RJR Fabrics; iron-on velour letters from Prym Consumer USA Inc.; ribbon from May Arts.*

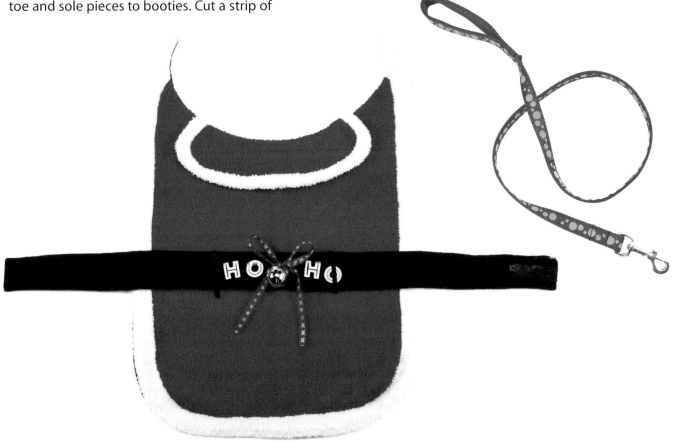

Mitering Instructions

Follow these steps to make perfect mitered corners.

Mitering Borders

Determining Length and Width

Mitering requires extra length for borders. Using the formula below, determine lengths needed for project borders.

Note: Examples use measurements from the tablecloth in Dress Up Your Table on page 36.

• Center length + (border width x 2) + 1 inch = length of side borders. ***Example:*** *68 inches + (10 inches x 2) + 1 inch = 89 inches.*

• Center width + (border width x 2) + 1 inch = length of end borders. ***Example:*** *44 inches + (10 inches x 2) + 1 inch = 65 inches.*

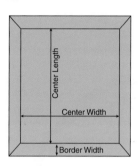

Figure 1

Cutting

Notes: Striped fabric or pieced borders, like the Dress Up Your Table tablecloth, should be cut so that the border designs are at right angles to the center of the tablecloth.

If your border is a solid color or an all-over print, it should be cut on the lengthwise grain of fabric so the border will have less stretch and more stability.

• Cut two each of the determined border measurements for length and width of project from your border material.

Assembly

1. Fold borders and center sides in half to determine center points and lightly press or mark with marking tool.

2. Pin two borders to center opposite sides with right sides together and center points matching.

Note: Borders will extend beyond corners of center.

3. Stitch together, beginning and ending the seam width (for example, ¼ inch) from the end of the center's corner (Figure 2).

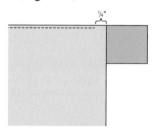

Figure 2

4. Repeat with end borders. Press seams toward borders. With wrong sides up, overlap borders at one corner (Figure 3).

Figure 3

5. Align ruler between the center corner point and where borders overlap. Draw a line connecting these points (Figure 4). This is the mitered seam line.

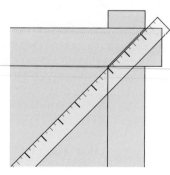

Figure 4

6. Place bottom border on top and repeat marking process (Figure 5).

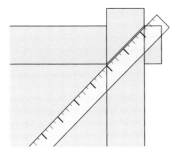

Figure 5

7. Place adjacent border strips right sides together. Match seam lines and pin along seam line (Figure 6). On a striped or pieced border, you must also check that the border pieces match at the seam lines.

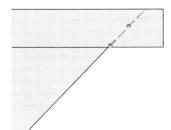

Figure 6

8. Begin stitching at the inside corner, following seam line exactly to outside corner. Check right side to see that corner lies flat (Figure 7).

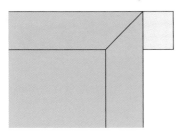

Figure 7

9. Trim seam and press open (Figure 8).

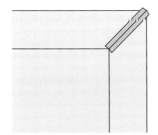

Figure 8

10. Repeat for all corners.

Mitering Double-Fold Hems

1. Press width of hem to wrong side of fabric on all edges, overlapping corner (Figure 9).

Figure 9

2. Fold corners over along a line that intersects where hem allowances meet (Figure 10).

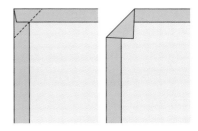

Figure 10

3. Turn second hem width to wrong side of fabric on all edges. Hem will form a miter at each corner (Figure 11). Pin to secure.

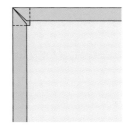

Figure 11

4. Begin edgestitching along one side. Pivot at each corner miter (Figure 12). Hand-stitch corners closed if hem allowance is wider than ½ inch. ❖

Figure 12

Meet the Designer

Carol Zentgraf is a freelance designer, writer and editor who specializes in sewing, fabrics and decorating. She also enjoys decorative painting, working with dyes, surface design on fabric and is an avid gardener. She has a degree in interior design and commercial art from Drake University and has worked in the craft and sewing industries as a product designer, magazine associate editor and book editor.

Carol has been a regular contributor to House of White Birches sewing books and is the author of *Pillows, Cushions and Tuffets, Decorative Storage, The Well-Dressed Window, Machine Embroidery Room-by-Room* and *Sewing for Outdoor Spaces*. Her designs and articles have also been published in a number of magazines.

Carol lives in Peoria, Ill., with her husband, Dave, and English bulldog, Lucy, and has two grown children, Dan and Carolyn.

Basic Sewing Supplies & Equipment

- Hand-sewing needles and thimble
- Marking pens or tailor's chalk
- Measuring tools: tape measure and ruler
- Pattern tracing paper or cloth
- Point turner
- Pressing tools: ham and point-turner boards
- Pressing equipment: board and iron, and press cloths
- Rotary cutter, mats and straightedges
- Scissors
- Sewing machine and matching thread

- Serger, if desired
- Straight pins and pincushion
- Spray adhesive (temporary)
- Seam sealant
- Seam ripper

See, Shop, Sew

Beacon Adhesives Inc.
(914) 699-3405
www.beaconcreates.com

Bonavista Fabrics
(800) 777-3877
www.bonavistafabrics.com

Clover Needlecraft Inc.
(800) 233-1703
www.clover-usa.com

Expo International
(800) 542-4367
www.expointl.com

Fabri-Quilt Inc.
(816) 421-2000
www.fabri-quilt.com

Fabric Café
(866) 855-0998
www.fabriccafe.com

Fairfield Processing
(800) 980-8000
www.poly-fil.com

Kandi Corp.
(727) 669-8000
www.kandicorp.com

Kwik Sew Pattern Co.
(888) 594-5739
www.kwiksew.com

May Arts
(206) 637-8366
www.mayarts.com

Michael Miller Fabrics
(212) 704-0774
www.michaelmiller
   fabrics.com

National Nonwovens
(800) 333-3469
www.national
   nonwovens.com

Prym Consumer USA Inc.
www.prymdritz.com

RJR Fabrics
(800) 422-5426
www.rjrfabrics.com

Robert Kaufman Fabrics
(800) 877-2066
www.robertkaufman.com

Sulky of America
(800) 874-4115
www.sulky.com

The Warm Company
(425) 248-2424
www.warmcompany.com

Waverly Fabrics
www.waverly.com

Metric Conversion Charts

Metric Conversions

Canada/U.S. Measurement		Multiplied by		Metric Measurement
yards	x	.9144	=	metres (m)
yards	x	91.44	=	centimetres (cm)
inches	x	2.54	=	centimetres (cm)
inches	x	25.40	=	millimetres (mm)
inches	x	.0254	=	metres (m)

Canada/U.S. Measurement		Multiplied by		Metric Measurement
centimetres	x	.3937	=	inches
metres	x	1.0936	=	yards

Standard Equivalents

Canada/U.S. Measurement		Metric Measurement		
⅛ inch	=	3.20 mm	=	0.32 cm
¼ inch	=	6.35 mm	=	0.635 cm
⅜ inch	=	9.50 mm	=	0.95 cm
½ inch	=	12.70 mm	=	1.27 cm
⅝ inch	=	15.90 mm	=	1.59 cm
¾ inch	=	19.10 mm	=	1.91 cm
⅞ inch	=	22.20 mm	=	2.22 cm
1 inches	=	25.40 mm	=	2.54 cm
⅛ yard	=	11.43 cm	=	0.11 m
¼ yard	=	22.86 cm	=	0.23 m
⅜ yard	=	34.29 cm	=	0.34 m
½ yard	=	45.72 cm	=	0.46 m
⅝ yard	=	57.15 cm	=	0.57 m
¾ yard	=	68.58 cm	=	0.69 m
⅞ yard	=	80.00 cm	=	0.80 m
1 yard	=	91.44 cm	=	0.91 m
1⅛ yards	=	102.87 cm	=	1.03 m
1¼ yards	=	114.30 cm	=	1.14 m

Canada/U.S. Measurement		Metric Measurement		
1⅜ yards	=	125.73 cm	=	1.26 m
1½ yards	=	137.16 cm	=	1.37 m
1⅝ yards	=	148.59 cm	=	1.49 m
1¾ yards	=	160.02 cm	=	1.60 m
1⅞ yards	=	171.44 cm	=	1.71 m
2 yards	=	182.88 cm	=	1.83 m
2⅛ yards	=	194.31 cm	=	1.94 m
2¼ yards	=	205.74 cm	=	2.06 m
2⅜ yards	=	217.17 cm	=	2.17 m
2½ yards	=	228.60 cm	=	2.29 m
2⅝ yards	=	240.03 cm	=	2.40 m
2¾ yards	=	251.46 cm	=	2.51 m
2⅞ yards	=	262.88 cm	=	2.63 m
3 yards	=	274.32 cm	=	2.74 m
3⅛ yards	=	285.75 cm	=	2.86 m
3¼ yards	=	297.18 cm	=	2.97 m
3⅜ yards	=	308.61 cm	=	3.09 m
3½ yards	=	320.04 cm	=	3.20 m
3⅝ yards	=	331.47 cm	=	3.31 m
3¾ yards	=	342.90 cm	=	3.43 m
3⅞ yards	=	354.32 cm	=	3.54 m
4 yards	=	365.76 cm	=	3.66 m
4⅛ yards	=	377.19 cm	=	3.77 m
4¼ yards	=	388.62 cm	=	3.89 m
4⅜ yards	=	400.05 cm	=	4.00 m
4½ yards	=	411.48 cm	=	4.11 m
4⅝ yards	=	422.91 cm	=	4.23 m
4¾ yards	=	434.34 cm	=	4.34 m
4⅞ yards	=	445.76 cm	=	4.46 m
5 yards	=	457.20 cm	=	4.57 m

E-mail: Customer_Service@whitebirches.com

HOUSE of WHITE BIRCHES
PUBLISHERS SINCE 1947

Sewing Season's Greetings is published by DRG, 306 East Parr Road, Berne, IN 46711, telephone (260) 589-4000. Printed in USA. Copyright © 2009 DRG. All rights reserved. This publication may not be reproduced in part or in whole without written permission from the publisher.

RETAIL STORES: If you would like to carry this pattern book or any other DRG publications, call the Wholesale Department at Annie's Attic to set up a direct account: (903) 636-4303. Also, request a complete listing of publications available from DRG.

Every effort has been made to ensure that the instructions in this pattern book are complete and accurate. We cannot, however, take responsibility for human error, typographical mistakes or variations in individual work.

STAFF

Editor: Diane Schmidt
Technical Editors: Angie Buckles, Marla Laux
Technical Artist: Nicole Gage
Copy Supervisor: Michelle Beck
Copy Editors: Amanda Ladig, Mary O'Donnell
Graphic Arts Supervisor: Ronda Bechinski

Graphic Artists: Glenda Chamberlain, Edith Teegarden
Art Director: Brad Snow
Assistant Art Director: Nick Pierce
Photography Supervisor: Tammy Christian
Photography: Matthew Owen
Photo Stylist: Tammy Steiner

ISBN: 978-1-59217-264-1

1 2 3 4 5 6 7 8 9

64

Photo Index

4

9

12

15

16

18

22

25

28

33

36

38

42

45

48

50

54

57

Sewing Season's Greetings